# Mediterranean Diet Cookbook For Weight Loss

## Easy and Delicious Recipes for Healthy Eating Every Day, Lose Weight and Decrease the Risk of Diseases

### Julia Miller

# Table of Contents

# Introduction

A Mediterranean diet combines the conventional healthy living practices of citizens from the Mediterranean Sea's neighboring countries like Italy, France, Spain, and Greece.

The Mediterranean diet differs from a country area, so it has a wide range of practices. It's high in fruits, vegetables, legumes, beans, nuts, grains, cereals, fish, and unsaturated fats like olive oil. Typically, it requires a moderate to low meat and dairy product consumption. This diet is not a fixed diet but instead an eating pattern inspired by the diet of Southern Europe's countries. The main focus is on fish, vegetables, olive oil, grains, beans, and poultry.

The Mediterranean diet is related to improved health and a healthy heart and body.

At least 16 nations surround the Mediterranean. Due to differences in religion, culture, economy, ethnic background, geography, and eating styles, agricultural production varies between these countries and even between regions.

It is widely agreed that people live longer in countries surrounding the Mediterranean Sea and experience fewer diseases, like cancer, and other chronic problems than other nations. The important factor is an active lifestyle, weight control, less sugar intake, low red meat and saturated fat consumption, and high in healthy foods and nuts. The Mediterranean diet can bring a variety of health benefits like heart and brain wellbeing, weight loss, cancer prevention, and the management of diabetes. You may still lose weight by adopting the Mediterranean diet and preventing serious illness.

You will attain a Mediterranean style diet by:

- Eating a lot of good starchy things, including pasta, whole wheat bread.

- Eating lots of vegetables, fruits, and fish.

- Consuming less red meat.

- Preferring items manufactured from the plant, vegetable oils, including olive oil.

The Mediterranean diet lifestyle requires low alcohol intake, non-smoking, physical exercise, good quality of sleep, weight loss, and efficient stress management. This diet favors lean protein, vegetables, herbs and fruits, omega-3 fatty acid diets, balanced fats, spices, and whole grains. It forbids processed goods, alcohol, and red meats. This diet is more of a healthy eating habit than a strict schedule.

# Will the Mediterranean Diet Help You Lose Weight?

The Mediterranean diet can help in losing weight and maintaining it. Although some people believe consuming a diet like the moderately fat-rich Mediterranean diet would make them overweight, many studies show the opposite is valid. It depends completely on which characteristics you follow and how you align it with your current lifestyle. For example, if you construct in your schedule a "calorie reduction," consuming fewer calories than the regular average limit or burning off more by exercising will make it possible for you to lose several pounds with the Mediterranean diet.

## Mediterranean Diet in the Food Pyramid

The healthy diet pyramid will help you start with the Mediterranean diet. This pyramid highlights eating veggies, beans, fruits, nuts, olive oil, whole grains, herbs, spices, and legumes to be eaten almost daily and seafood some times a week, at the very least, eggs, poultry, yogurt, and cheese in balance, while leaving desserts and red meat for special occasions. Alcohol consumption should be very minimum, and the most important part is to stay active and do physical activity.

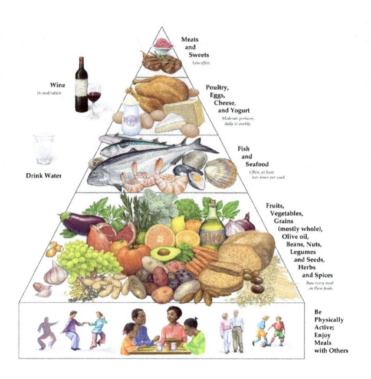

The pyramid of the Mediterranean diet was based on how Mediterranean people eat. They follow this pyramid guideline on what to eat and when to eat, along with having an active, healthy lifestyle. The benefits of following the Mediterranean food pyramid brings are lower risk of dementia and fewer memory disorders, reduced chance of having a stroke, diabetes, and prevent vascular diseases. According to this food pyramid, your meal should have these ingredients and in this specific order of priority.

## Eat Daily

- Vegetables and fruits (because of the antioxidants)

- Nuts, legumes, whole grains, beans

---

12

- Olive oil as the main source of fat

## Eat Twice a Week

- Seafood and fish

## Eat Moderately Daily to Weekly

- Poultry

- Eggs, dairy, and cheese

- Red wine (one glass per day)

## Avoid These Unhealthy Foods

Must avoid these foods while following the Mediterranean diet:

- Saturated fat

- Red meat

- Desserts

- Processed meats like hot dogs and sausages

- Sugars such as ice cream, Soda, table sugar, and candies

- Trans fats such as those found in processed foods like margarine

- Refined oils like canola oil, soybean oil, and cottonseed oil

- Refined grains such as refined wheat, pasta, and whole wheat bread

- Highly processed foods like those factory-made, and food labeled as low-fat or diet

# What to Eat in the Mediterranean Diet?

A Mediterranean-style diet includes:

- Plenty of vegetables, fruits, grains, bread, potatoes, beans, seeds, and nuts

- Olive oil

- Dairy products, fish, poultry, eggs, moderately

- Fruit as a dessert instead of sweets

## Main Ingredients to Shop For

Here are some examples of ingredients that people often include in the Mediterranean diet:

- **Vegetables**: peppers, eggplant, tomatoes, leafy green vegetables, onions, zucchini, cucumbers, potatoes, and sweet potatoes

- **Poultry**: mainly turkey and chicken

- **Berries**: blueberries and strawberries

- **Fruits**: apples, melon, peaches, apricots, lemons, oranges

- **Nuts and seeds**: walnuts, almonds, cashews, and sunflower seeds

- **Unsaturated fats**: sunflower oil, olive oil, avocados, and olives

- **Dairy products**: yogurt, cheese

- **Legumes**: lentils, chickpeas, and beans

- **Seeds**: pumpkin seeds and sunflower seeds

- **Fish**: oily fish, sardines, shellfish, and oysters

- **Eggs:** duck eggs, chicken, omega-3 enriched and quail eggs

- **Drinks**: red wine

- **All kinds of herbs and spices:** nutmeg, basil, garlic, peppermint, sage, rosemary, cinnamon

These foods are rich in fiber, vitamins, minerals, healthy fats, antioxidants, and have low sugar levels.

# Benefits of the Mediterranean Diet

- The Mediterranean diet will help you immensely in losing weight and maintaining it.

- By preparing and freezing meals in advance, you can save time with the Mediterranean diet.

- Hunger shouldn't be a concern with this diet because it is so fulfilling.

- A Mediterranean diet can help prevent cardiac diseases, some tumors, dementia, and cognitive disability.

- This dietary pattern will play a major role in avoiding heart and lung disease and reducing risk factors of diabetes, obesity, high blood pressure, and elevated cholesterol. There is some indication that a Mediterranean diet high in virgin olive oil will help the body eliminate extra cholesterol from the arteries and keep blood channels clear.

- You will be more agile. In any older adult, if following Mediterranean diet, nutrients will decrease the likelihood of experiencing muscle weakening and symptoms of feebleness by around seventy percent.

- You will reduce the risk of getting Alzheimer's disease, research indicates that this diet can boost good cholesterol, improve sugar levels in the blood, and improve blood vessels' health.

- These healthy blood vessels will reduce the risk of dementia as well.

- Lower the possibilities of getting Parkinson's disease. The high amounts of antioxidants in the ingredients will prevent the human body's cells not to go through a harmful mechanism known as oxidative stress, hence reducing the risk of Parkinson's disease.

- Good life quality by reducing the chance of coronary disease and cancer with the help of this diet, you will reduce the risk of dying through 21% at any age.

- Protection from type 2 diabetes. This diet is high in fiber and digests food slowly, avoids massive spikes of blood sugar.

- This Mediterranean diet can help you hold your weight stable for a longer period.

# Mediterranean Breakfast Recipes

If you try the Mediterranean diet, you realize that you can fill your plate with veggies and healthy proteins for you, including salmon. Then what for breakfast? Apple, cheese, and whole grains play a significant part in the diet, but literally, there are lots of delicious breakfast recipes to choose from. Breakfasts of the Mediterranean diet will sustain you till lunch.

## 1.Caprese Avocado Toast

(**Ready in:** 20 minutes | **Serving:** 2)

**Ingredients**

- Grape tomatoes: 8 pieces (halved)

- Whole grain bread: 2 slices

- Fresh ciliegine or mozzarella balls: 4 tbsp.

- Fresh basil leaves

- Avocado: one medium (pitted)

- Balsamic glaze: 2 tbsp.

**Instructions**

1. Mash the avocado in a bowl and toast the bread.

2. Over the toasted bread, spread the mashed avocado.

3. Top each slice of toasted bread with mozzarella balls, basil leaves, and tomatoes.

4. While serving, drizzle with balsamic glaze.

5. Enjoy.

**Nutritional value**: Calories 649 | Fat 24.6 g | Saturated 6.6 g | Carbs 86.4 g | Protein 10.5 g

# 2.Eggs with Zucchini, Bell Peppers, and Summer Tomatoes

(**Ready in**: 20 minutes | **Serving:** 2)

**Ingredients**

- One tsp. of Spanish paprika

- Olive oil: 1 tbsp.

- One clove of minced garlic

- Zucchini: 4 cups

- Yellow onion: one (sliced)

- One red bell pepper

- Two eggs

- Salt and pepper to taste

- Half tsp. of fresh thyme

- Tomatoes: 3 cups, chopped

## Instructions

1. Heat olive oil over medium flame in a skillet.

2. Add onion cook for five minutes. Then add the garlic cook for one minute.

3. Add zucchini and cook for ten minutes, until it starts to soften.

4. Add thyme, tomatoes, and paprika. Let it cook for another 20 minutes until it is thick.

5. Meanwhile, roast pepper on low flame. Once it is charred, remove the center and seeds, and cut it into one-inch pieces.

6. Turn off the heat, add the pepper, salt, and roasted peppers.

7. Serve hot or warm topped with eggs.

**Nutritional value:**Calories 226 | Fat 2.5 g | Carbs 20.6 g | Protein 11.1g

# 3.Sweet Potato Breakfast Patties

(**Ready in:** 20 minutes | **Serving:** 2)

## Ingredients

- Sweet potato: 1/4 cup (steamed)

- One egg

- 4 tbsp. of cooked lentils

- One tsp. of cinnamon

- 4 tbsp. of yogurt

- ¼ cup of blueberries

- 4 tbsp. of banana

## Instructions

1. First off, mash the banana and sweet potato gently with a masher, mix in the egg well.

2. Then add the lentils in it, and add the cinnamon. Mix it all well.

3. Put a heavy skillet over medium flame. Pour a spoonful of mixture in it. The size of the patties depends on your liking.

4. Let the patties cook on a medium flame for three minutes each side.

5. Top with blueberries, yogurt, and serve warm.

**Nutritional value**:Calories 449 | Fat 21.6g | Carbs 36.4g | Protein 10.5g

# 4.Spanish Omelet

(**Ready in:** 20 minutes | **Serving:** 2)

## Ingredients

- ¼ cup of parsley, (finely diced)

- Five eggs

- One onion (sliced)

- 4 tbsp. of olive oil

- Half red bell pepper: chopped

- ¼ tsp. of sea salt

- Baby potatoes: 1¼ cups (¼-inch slices)

- ¼ tsp. of freshly ground black pepper

## Instructions

1. Put a heavy skillet over medium flame. Add two tablespoons of olive oil, then add the onion, bell pepper, and potatoes and cover and cook for around 15 minutes, stirring the onion and potatoes every five minutes, until the potatoes are tender and soft.

2. In the meantime, beat the eggs in a big bowl with parsley. Season with salt and pepper.

3. In a bowl, add the mixture of potato with the eggs and mix well. With the help of a paper towel, clean the sauté pan.

4. Put the same skillet over medium flame, then add the other two spoons of olive oil. Pour the mixture of potato and egg into the skillet and cover, lower the heat to medium-low, and simmer for about five minutes.

5. When the eggs are almost done, and the bottom is mildly brown, put the omelet onto a tray, then slip it back into the pan and let it cook for five minutes more.

6. Put it back onto a plate until the bottom is light brown and top with fresh parsley.

7. Serve right away.

**Nutritional value**: Calories 319 | Fat 14.6 g | Carbs 26 g | Protein 15 g

# 5.Poached Eggs Caprese

(**Ready in:** 20 minutes | **Serving:** 2)

## Ingredients

- One thickly sliced tomato

- White vinegar: 1 tbsp. (distilled)

- English muffins: 2 (split)

- Salt: 2 tsp.

- Mozzarella cheese: 4 slices

- Pesto: 4 tsp.

- One pinch of salt or to taste

- Four eggs

## Instructions

1. Load a large saucepan with two-three inches of water and let it boil over a high flame.

2. Lower the heat to medium, add in the vinegar, and two tsp. of salt and let the water simmer, lightly.

3. Meanwhile, put a slice of thick tomato and mozzarella cheese slice on each English muffin split, then toast in an oven so that the cheese will soften and the English muffin will be toasted for around five minutes.

4. Crack one egg into a small bowl.

5. Keep the bowl just above the water level, and softly drop the egg into the water. Repeat the same process with other eggs.

6. Poach the eggs for almost three minutes until the whites are vibrant in color, and the yolks are medium-hard. Using a slotted spoon to extract the bowl's eggs, pat on a kitchen towel to eliminate extra water.

7. Put one poached egg on top of every piece of English muffin.

8. Top with a spoonful of pesto and salt to taste, and serve.

**Nutritional value**: Calories 482.1 | Fat 24.9 g | Carbs 31.7 g | Protein 33.3 g

# 6.Breakfast Pita Pizza

(**Ready in:** 55 minutes | **Serving:** 2)

**Ingredients**

- Fresh mushrooms: ¼ cup (diced)

- Bacon: 4 slices

- Half a cup chopped spinach

- Onion: ¼ and chopped

- Pesto: 2 tbsp.

- Four beaten large eggs

- Pita bread rounds: 2 pieces

- Half a cup Cheddar cheese (shredded)

- Olive oil: 2 tbsp. (extra virgin)

- Half of a tomato (diced)

- One avocado (pitted, sliced, and peeled)

**Instructions**

1. Let the oven pre-heat to 350 F. Put a parchment paper on a baking tray.

2. Put the bacon in a wide skillet and cook over medium flame, frequently turning until well browned for around ten minutes. With the help of a paper towel, absorb excess oil.

3. Add onions in the same skillet and cook for about five minutes, until smooth and translucent. Turn off the heat, put onions to the side.

4. Add olive oil in the skillet, add in the eggs and cook for five minutes, frequently stirring until cooked thoroughly.

5. Add pita bread to the baking pan. Pesto scattered over pita; add bacon on pita, scrambled eggs, spinach, mushroom, and onions.

6. Add shredded cheddar cheese on top.

7. Let it bake in the oven for about ten minutes, until the cheese has melted.

8. Top with parsley and serve immediately.

**Nutritional value**: Calories 873.2 | Fat 62.9 g | Carbs 43.5 g | Protein 36.8 g

# 7.Egg and Tomato Shakshuka

(**Ready in:** 20 minutes | **Serving:** 2)

**Ingredients**

- Olive Oil: 1-2 Teaspoons (Extra Virgin)

- Half Of A Red Onion (Finely Diced)

- One Orange Bell Pepper (Diced)

- One Red Bell Pepper (Diced)

- One Zucchini (Diced)

- Tomatoes: One Can

- Two Springs Of Parsley (Diced)

- ¼ Tsp. Of Cayenne Pepper

- ¼ Tsp. Of Smoked Paprika

- One Cup Of Spinach, Chopped (Fresh Or Frozen)

- Brussels Sprouts: 5-6 Pieces (Finely Diced)

- Half A Cup Of Light Stock

- Four Eggs

- Salt And Pepper To Taste

- Red Pepper Flakes And Lemon Zest (For Serving)

## Instructions

1. In A Deep, Large Skillet, Heat The Olive Oil Over Medium To High Flame.

2. Add The Zucchini, Peppers, Brussels Sprouts, Onion, And Spinach To The Pan With Salt And Pepper To Taste, For Five Minutes Until The Onion Is Translucent.

3. Then Add The Smoked Paprika, Cayenne Pepper, And Half The Chopped Parsley Together.

4. Add In The Tomatoes, Then Add The Chicken Stock And Let It Simmer Gently. Cook For Almost Five Minutes.

5. Create A Small Divot, Where You Will Put The Egg Softly.

6. Crack One Egg Into A Tiny Cup, Then Pour Into The Divot Carefully. Repeat The Divot Process With Every Egg.

7. Cook For Around Three Minutes Until The Egg Whites Are Solid While The Yolk Is Loose On The Inside.

8. Top With Remaining Parsley, Lemon Zest, And Red Pepper Flakes.

**Nutritional value**: Calories 327 | Fat 22 g | Carbs 32 g | Protein 23 g

# 8.Vegan Green Shakshuka

(**Ready in**: 30 minutes | **Serving:** 2)

**Ingredients**

- One can of cannellini beans

- One leek

- Half cup of fresh mint leaves

- One avocado (ripened)

- Two minced cloves of garlic

- Half cup of fresh parsley leaves

- Three and a ½ tbsp. of yogurt (plant-based)

- Half cup of fresh dill

- One tablespoon of olive oil

- Half a tsp. of za'atar

- One and a half cups of frozen peas

- ¼ cup of fresh spinach leaves

- Crusty whole-wheat bread: 4 slices

- Salt and freshly ground black pepper to taste

**Instructions**

1. Cut the leek into thin pieces and trim it before slicing. Mince the peeled garlic.

2. Drain the water and rinse the cannellini beans.

3. Finely dice the dill, mint, and parsley. Cut and halve the avocado gently. Scoop out and dice the avocado.

4. In a wide skillet, heat the olive oil over medium flame.

5. Cook the leek slices, frequently stirring for five minutes, until tender.

6. Lower the heat, then add the garlic, let it cook for another minute.

7. Add the peas and beans and cook for two minutes.

8. Then add one handful at a time the spinach, stirring frequently and letting every batch of spinach wilt down before you add the next until all the spinach has wilted down and the peas are fully thawed and cooked, then turn off the heat.

9. Stir in the parsley, dill, and mint, season with pepper, and salt to your liking.

10. Garnish with za'atar, sliced avocado, yogurt, and crusty whole wheat bread

**Nutritional value**: Calories 257 | Fat 20 g | Carbs 19.9 g | Protein 26 g

# 9.Spinach Artichoke Frittata

(**Ready in:** 25 minutes | **Serving:** 4-6)

**Ingredients**

- Two tbsp. of olive oil

- Ten large eggs

- One tbsp. of Dijon mustard

- One tsp. of kosher salt

- Two cloves of diced garlic

- Half a cup full-fat sour cream

- Baby spinach: 5 packed cups

- One cup of Parmesan cheese (grated, divided)

- One and a half cup of marinated artichoke hearts (quarter)

- 1/4 teaspoon of freshly ground black pepper

**Instructions**

1.  Let the oven heat to 400F with a rack in the middle.

2.  Put the sour cream, eggs, half cup of grated parmesan, mustard, pepper, and salt in a big bowl and mix with whisker; set it aside.

3.  Heat the oil over medium flame in a cast-iron skillet or oven-safe nonstick pan until it shines.

4.  Place the artichokes in one layer and fry, frequently stirring for 6- 8 minutes, until nicely browned.

5.  Add garlic and spinach and shake for around two minutes before the spinach is wilted, and nearly all the liquid is evaporated.

6.  Spread all this out into one even sheet. Pour the mixture of eggs over the vegetables. Sprinkle with the half a cup of Parmesan cheese.

7.  Move the saucepan to make sure that the eggs spread equally over all vegetables. Cook for three minutes, untouched, until the eggs start to set at the sides.

8.  Bake for 12- 15 minutes, until the eggs are completely cooked.

9. Cut a tiny slice into the middle of the frittata to check. If the raw eggs pass through the cut, bake for a couple more minutes. Cool for five minutes in the pan, then slice and serve hot.

**Nutritional value**: Calories 316 | Fat 25.9g | Carbs 6.4g | Protein 17.9 g

# 10.Mediterranean Breakfast Quinoa

(**Ready in:** 20 minutes | **Serving:** 4)

**Ingredients**

- Milk: 2 cups

- Two diced, dried dates (pitted)

- Quinoa: one cup

- Sea salt: One tsp.

- Ground cinnamon: one tsp.

- Vanilla extract: one tsp.

- Five diced, dried apricots

- Honey: 2 tbsp.

- Two diced, dried dates (pitted)

**Instructions**

1. Add the almonds in a skillet over medium flame, let them toast for 3-5 minutes, then set it aside.

2. Put a saucepan over medium flame, add in the quinoa and cinnamon, heat until it's all warmed up.

3. Add in the sea salt, milk, and mix, let it boil.

4. Lower the heat, cover the saucepan and let it simmer for 15 minutes.

5. Add in the dates, apricot, honey, vanilla, and half the almonds in the quinoa mix.

6. Garnish with the rest of the almonds.

7. Serve immediately.

**Nutritional value**: Calories 213 | Fat 14.2 g | Carbs 22 g | Protein 17 g

# 11.Mediterranean Breakfast Pitas

(**Ready in:** 40 minutes | **Serving:** 4)

## Ingredients

- Hot sauce (optional)

- Four large eggs

- Freshly ground black pepper

- Half a cup of hummus

- Salt, to taste

- Two medium tomatoes, roughly chopped

- One medium cucumber sliced into thin rounds

- One cup of fresh parsley leaves, roughly chopped

- Whole-wheat pita bread with pockets: 2 pieces, cut in half

## Instructions

1. Add water in a saucepan and let it boil.

2. Place your room temperature eggs in the water and cook for 7-8 minutes.

3. After the eggs have boiled, drain the water and add cold water to the pan with the boiled eggs to cool them down.

4. After 3-4 minutes, peel the eggs and slice them into 1/4 thin slices, season with pepper and salt.

5. Add two tbsp. of hummus in each whole-wheat pita bread slices' pocket.

6. Add few roughly chopped tomatoes and the cucumber slices in each pocket.

7. Add pepper and salt.

8. Add one sliced egg into pita bread pocket, garnish with hot sauce and parsley. Enjoy.

**Nutritional value**: Calories 206 | Fat 8.3g | Carbs 22.9g | Protein 12.0 g

# 12. Banana Split Yogurt

(**Ready in:** 5 minutes | **Serving:** 2)

## Ingredients

- 1/2 tsp. of strawberry jam

- Greek yogurt: one cup (plain flavored)

- 1/2 teaspoon of cacao nibs

- Half of a banana (sliced)

## Instructions

1.  Add the plain Greek yogurt in a bowl.

2.  Top with cacao nibs, strawberry jam, and banana slices on top.

3.  Mix all together and enjoy it.

**Nutritional value**: Calories 150 | Fat 12 g | Carbs 6.6 g | Protein 9 g

# Mediterranean Lunch Recipes

Mediterranean diet is deemed one of the healthiest diets. Those who adopt it are less prone to experience a high level of cholesterol, elevated blood pressure, or become overweight. It is, however, a great way to feast. Pick up these recipes for effective Mediterranean diets and stay safe all week long.

## 1.Mediterranean Lettuce Wraps

(**Ready in:** 10 minutes | **Serving:** 4)

**Ingredients**

- Lettuce leaves: 12 pieces large

- ¼ of a cup tahini

- One teaspoon of lemon zest

- ¼ of a cup lemon juice

- Half teaspoon of paprika

- ¼ of a cup extra-virgin olive oil

- Half of a cup of shallots (thinly sliced)

- ¾ of a teaspoon of kosher salt

- Two cans unsalted chickpeas, (15 ounces each, rinsed)

- Half of a cup of sliced jarred roasted red peppers (drained)

- Half of a cup of shallots (thinly sliced)

- One and a ½ teaspoons of maple syrup (pure)

- ¼ of a cup chopped almonds, (preferably toasted)

- Two tablespoons of fresh parsley (chopped)

## Instructions

1. In a big mix mixing bowl, whisk together lemon zest, maple syrup, tahini, paprika, oil, lemon juice, and salt.

2. Add shallots, chickpeas and peppers. Mix to coat well.

3. Take big lettuce leaves and on each leaf, add this mixture about 1/3 of a cup. Garnish with toasted almonds and parsley. Then, wrap the filling in lettuce leaves.

4. Serve right away and enjoy it.

**Nutritional value**: Calories 498 | Fat 28 g | Carbs 43.7 g | Protein 15.8 g

# 2.Mediterranean Chicken Quinoa Bowl

(**Ready in:** 30 minutes | **Serving:** 4)

## Ingredients

- ¼ of a tsp. of salt

- ¼ of a cup of feta cheese(crumbled)

- One teaspoon of paprika

- ¼ of cup of almonds (sliced)

- 4 tbsp. of divided, extra-virgin olive oil

- One small clove garlic, minced

- Half of a tsp. of ground cumin

- 2 cups quinoa (cooked)

- ¼ of a cup pitted Kalamata olives, diced

- ¼ of a cup red onion (thinly sliced)

- 1 cup diced cucumber

- ¼ of a tsp. of freshly ground black pepper

- Two tablespoons thinly sliced fresh parsley

- ¼ of a teaspoon crushed red pepper (optional)

- One jar of roasted red peppers, rinsed (17 ounces)

- Boneless, chicken breasts: 4 cups (trimmed and skinless)

## Instructions

1. In the upper third of the oven, put a rack, preheat the broiler to high. Place foil on a rimmed baking dish.

2. Add salt and pepper to the chicken, and put on the baking sheet. Let it broil, rotating once, until an instant-read thermometer, if inserted in the thickest section, registers 165 F, for almost 18 minutes.

3. Place the chicken on a cutting board. Cut into slices or shred with forks.

4. Meanwhile, place peppers, crushed red pepper, almonds, paprika, two spoonsful of oil, cumin, and garlic in a food processor.

5. Pulse on high until creamy.

6. In a medium dish, mix quinoa, red onion, and olives add the remaining two tablespoons of oil.

7. Take four bowls, and divide the quinoa among these bowls, and finish with similar quantities of chicken, cucumber, and red pepper sauce.

8. Sprinkle with feta and parsley

**Nutritional value**: Calories 519 | Fat 26.9g | Carbs 31.2g | Protein 34.1g

# 3.Tomato Salad with Grilled Halloumi and Herbs

(**Ready in:** 25 minutes | **Serving:** 2)

## Ingredients

- Basil: 5 leaves, chopped

- 4 cups of round sliced tomatoes

- Sea salt

- Freshly ground black pepper

- Half of a lemon

- Extra-virgin olive oil

- Finely sliced flat-leaf parsley: 2 tablespoons

- 2 cups of halloumi cheese (4 slabs, cut in slices)

## Instructions

1. Let the grill pre-heat or put grill pan over medium flame.

2. Take four plates, arrange the tomatoes slices on a serving platter. Season with salt and freshly ground black pepper with lemon juice on top.

3. Then oil the grill and add halloumi and let cook, until grill marks appear or the cheese is thoroughly warmed, cook each side for almost one minute.

4. Put this warmed cheese over tomatoes.

5. Add extra-virgin olive oil and sprinkle with the parsley and basil. Serve right away and enjoy it.

**Nutritional value**: Calories 196 | Fat 15 g | Carbs 8 g | Protein 9 g

# 4.Harissa Marinated Chicken Tenders

(**Ready in:** about 40 minutes | **Serving:** 4)

## Ingredients

- Plain Greek yogurt: ¼ cup

- Harissa paste: 2 tablespoons

- Boneless, skinless chicken: 8 cups (18-24 tenders)

- Dry white wine: ¼ cup

## Instructions

1. Put harissa, yogurt, and wine together in a baking dish, put the chicken tenders, and cover with the yogurt mixture. Cover with wrap, put it in the refrigerator. Marinate for two hours or so before midnight.

2. Fire up the grill. Take out the chicken from the marinade to make any excess drip away. Put the chicken on the hot grill, and cook on either side for around 5 minutes.

3. Serve with a side bowl of rice, couscous, quinoa, or a sandwich. With herbs and sautéed vegetables.

**Nutritional value:** Calories 206 | Fat 18.7 g | Carbs 21 g | Protein 20.1 g

# 5.Moroccan Harissa Chickpea Stew with Eggplant and Millet

(**Ready in:** 20 minutes | **Serving**: 2)

**Ingredients**

- Three cloves of garlic (minced)

- Millet: one cup

- Freshly ground black pepper

- Japanese eggplant: one large

- One medium onion (chopped)

- One can puree tomatoes (14 ounces)

- Harissa paste: 2 tablespoons

- For garnish, one bunch of cilantro

- Kosher salt, to taste

- Two tablespoons of ghee (or extra-virgin olive oil) divided

## Instructions

1. Add two cups of water with salt in a big saucepan, let it boil, then add millet. Let it boil again and cover, simmer for almost 25 minutes.

2. When cooking is completely done, remove the cover, with a fork, fluff it, and cool it.

3. In the meantime, in a large skillet, heat one tablespoon of extra virgin olive oil over medium flame.

4. Add the eggplant, adjust seasoning with salt and pepper, and cook for around ten minutes until soft and light brown, add more ghee if required, to keep the eggplant from sticking to the skillet.

5. Move the eggplant to a bowl and put it aside.

6. To the same pan, add the remaining tbsp. of ghee, then add onion and cook for ten minutes, until translucent and soft.

7. Stir in the garlic and cook for another two minutes. Season with salt and pepper, then add the harissa, chickpeas, and tomatoes.

8. Turn the heat low and add the eggplant. Let it simmer for 10-15 minutes.

9. Take two bowls, add the millet into each bowl and finish with the stew.

10. Top with cilantro leaves and serve hot.

**Nutritional value**: Calories 600 | Fat 15 g | Carbs 211 g | Protein 20 g

# 6.Salmon Pita Sandwich

(**Ready in**: 10 minutes | **Serving:** 1)

**Ingredients**

- Whole-wheat pita bread: half (6 inches)

- Chopped fresh dill: 2 teaspoons

- Half of a teaspoon prepared horseradish

- Nonfat yogurt: 2 tablespoons (plain)

- Lemon juice: 2 tsp.

- Half of a cup of watercress

- Flaked canned sockeye salmon: 6 tbsp. (drained)

**Instructions**

1. In a small mixing bowl, mix lemon juice, yogurt, horseradish, and dill.

2. Mix well.

3. Add in the salmon.

4. Put the salmon salad into a pita pocket with watercress.

5. Serve right away, enjoy.

**Nutrition value**: Calories 239 | Fat 7.1 g | Carbs 19 g | Protein 24.8 g

# 7.Hummus and Greek Salad

(**Ready in:** 10 minutes | **Serving:** 1)

## Ingredients

- Arugula: 2 cups

- ⅓ of a cup cucumber (sliced)

- Diced red onion: one tablespoon

- Feta cheese: 1 tablespoon (crumbled)

- ⅓ of a cup halved cherry tomatoes

- 4-inch whole-wheat pita: one piece

- ¼ of a cup hummus

- One and a ½ tablespoon of extra-virgin olive oil

- ⅛ of a teaspoon freshly ground black pepper

- Two teaspoons of red-wine vinegar

## Instructions

1. In a big mixing bowl, add onion, arugula, tomatoes, black pepper, cucumber, oil, and vinegar.

2. Mix well.

3. Add feta on top.

4. Serve with hummus and pita bread slices.

5. Enjoy.

**Nutritional value**: Calories 422 | Fat 29.9g | Carbs 30.5g | Protein 10.9g

# 8.Grilled Lemon Herb Chicken and Avocado Salad

(**Ready in:** 25 minutes | **Serving:** 4)

**Ingredients**

- Boneless, chicken breasts: 6 cups (skinless)

- Chopped fresh dill: 1 tablespoon

- Extra-virgin olive oil: 3 tablespoons

- Chopped fresh oregano: 1 tablespoon

- Kosher salt and freshly ground black pepper

- Juice of 2 lemons, and zest

- Chopped fresh parsley: 3 tablespoons

**Salad**

- Chicken broth: 2 and a ½ cups

- Barley: 1 cup

- Juice of 1 lemon and zest

- ⅓ of a cup extra-virgin olive oil

- One halved red onion (thinly sliced)

- Whole-grain mustard: 1 tablespoon

- One pint of cherry tomatoes (diced)

- 2 avocados, cut in slices

- 2 heads of red-leaf lettuce (diced)

- Dried oregano: 1 teaspoon

- Kosher salt and freshly ground black pepper

## Instructions

1. To make Lemon Herb Chicken, put the chicken inside a large plastic sealed plastic bag. In a bowl, add lemon juice, olive oil, dill, lemon zest, parsley, and oregano and mix well.

2. Then pour this marinade into the sealed bag, seal, and chill for almost half an hour.

3. In the meantime, put the chicken broth and barley over medium flame in a saucepan and let it simmer.

4. Cover the pot and steam until the barley is soft for almost 30-45 minutes. Drain and set it aside.

5. Mix the oregano lemon juice, lemon zest, and mustard in a bowl, then slowly drizzle in the olive oil and mix properly. Add salt and pepper to taste.

6. Let your grill pre-heat at high. Take chicken out from marinade and sprinkle with freshly ground black pepper and salt.

7. Grill the chicken on each side until charred and completely cooked through, cook for almost ten minutes, flipping as required, take the chicken from the grill and set it aside.

8. In a big bowl, mix the onion, tomato, and lettuce, drizzle the dressing and coat well.

9. Cut the chicken into slices and put at the top of the salad with avocado slices.

**Nutritional value**: **Lemon-Herb Chicken**

Calories 309 | Fat 14 g | Carbs 4 g | Protein 39 g

**Salad :** Calories 602 | Fat 36 g | Carbs 60 g | Protein 15 g

# 9.Mediterranean Wraps

(**Ready in:** 40 minutes | **Serving:** 4)

**Ingredients**

- Tortillas

- Extra-virgin olive oil: 3 tablespoons

- One cup of chopped fresh parsley

- Half of a cup water

- ¼ of a cup lemon juice

- Minced garlic: 2 teaspoons

- Fine salt: ¼ teaspoon, divided

- 4 cups of chicken tenders

- One medium tomato, diced

- ¼ of a teaspoon freshly ground black pepper

- ⅓ of a cup couscous (preferably whole-wheat)

- Half of a cup chopped fresh mint leaves

- One cup of diced cucumber

## Instructions

1. Add water to a deep saucepan. Let it boil. Add the couscous and turn off the heat, cover and let it rest for five minutes.

2. With a fork, fluff it. Set it aside.

3. In the meantime, mix mint, parsley, lemon juice, garlic, oil, 1/8 teaspoon of salt, and pepper in a mixing bowl.

4. Mix the chicken tenders, with one tbsp. of parsley mix and add the 1/8 tsp. of salt.

5. Put the tenders in a wide non-stick skillet and cook over medium flame until cooked completely for almost five minutes each side. Move to a cutting surface.

6. Chop into bite-size bits after it's cooled down enough to cut.

7. Add the leftover parsley mixture to the couscous with cucumber and tomato.

8. On each wrap, put about 3/4 of the couscous mix and Divide equally the chicken in the wraps.

9. Pull the wraps up like a burrito, tucking in the sides to keep the ingredients in. Cut in half and serve right away and enjoy.

**Nutritional value**: Calories 519 | Fat 17.5g | Carbs 54.9g | Protein 32.2g

# 10.Mediterranean Bento Lunch

(**Ready in:** 15 minutes | **Serving:** 1)

**Ingredients**

- One pita bread (whole-wheat, quartered)

- ¼ of a cup rinsed chickpeas

- ¼ of a cup chopped tomato

- Chopped olives: 1 tablespoon

- Grapes: one cup

- Crumbled feta cheese: 1 tablespoon

- ¼ of a cup chopped cucumber

- Chopped fresh parsley: 1 tablespoon

- Extra-virgin olive oil: half teaspoon

- Red-wine vinegar: 1 teaspoon

- 1 and 1/2 cup of grilled turkey breast tenderloin

- Hummus: 2 tablespoons

**Instructions**

1. In a mixing bowl, add tomato, feta, cucumber, olives, vinegar, oil, chickpeas, and parsley and toss well until well combined.

2. Put this mixture in a dish.

3. Put turkey or chicken (if using) in another dish.

4. Add pita, hummus, and grapes side by side in small containers.

5. Serve all these together in a lunch box or a box with different containers.

6. Pack it away and enjoy it later.

**Nutritional value**: Calories 497 | Fat 13.8g | Carbs 60.5g | Protein 36.7g

# 11.5-Minute Heirloom Tomato and Cucumber Toast

(**Ready in:** 5 minutes | **Serving:** 1)

**Ingredients**

- Whole Grain Crispbread: 2 pieces

- Extra-virgin olive oil: 1 teaspoon

- A pinch of dried oregano

- One Persian cucumber, chopped

- Kosher salt

- Freshly ground black pepper

- Balsamic glaze: 1 teaspoon

- Heirloom tomato: one small, chopped

- Whipped cream cheese: 2 teaspoons (low-fat)

**Instructions**

1. Mix the cucumber, tomato, oregano, olive oil, and season with salt and freshly ground black pepper in a small mixing bowl.

2. Spread the cream cheese on slices of bread add on top the cucumber, tomato mixture drizzle with balsamic glaze.

3. Serve right away and enjoy it.

**Nutritional value**: Calories 177 | Fat 8 g | Carbs 24 g | Protein 3 g

# 12.Greek Chicken and Rice Skillet

(**Ready in**: 30 minutes | **Serving:** 4)

**Ingredients**

- Green olives: 1 cup

- Six pieces of chicken thighs

- Chicken broth: 2 and a ½ cups

- Long-grain rice: 1 cup

- Dried oregano: 1 teaspoon

- Garlic powder: 1 teaspoon

- Three lemons

- Extra-virgin olive oil: 2 tablespoons

- Half of a cup crumbled feta cheese

- Half red onion, chopped

- 2 cloves of minced garlic

- ⅓ of a cup fresh chopped fresh parsley

- Chopped fresh oregano: 1 tablespoon (more for garnishing)

- Kosher salt and freshly ground black pepper

**Instructions**

1. Let the oven pre-heat to 375°F.

2. Add salt and pepper to chicken thighs, and mix garlic powder, dried oregano, zest of one lemon in a small mixing bowl, rub this mixture on chicken thighs generously.

3. In a wide skillet, heat the olive oil over medium flame. Put the meat, skin side down, then sear for nine minutes until the meat turns light brown. Move to the plate and set aside.

4. Add the garlic and onion in the pan, and sauté for around five minutes until opaque. Add the rice and sauté for one minute; then season with salt.

5. Add the broth and let it boil then slow to simmer. Add the zest and lemon juice, and the oregano. Cut two slices for later.

6. Put the chicken skin side down into the rice. Put the skillet in a pre-heated oven till all the broth is absorbed, and chicken is thoroughly cooked, for almost 25 minutes.

7. Now turn the broiler, and put the lemon slices on the chicken. Broil until the lemons are finely crispy, and the chicken skin is also crispy, for almost three minutes.

8.  Then add the feta and olives over the lemon slices, top with parsley leaves, and serve hot.

**Nutritional value:** Calories 903 | Fat 55 g | Carbs 54 g | Protein 48 g

# 13.Greek Chicken and Cucumber Pita Sandwiches with Yogurt Sauce

(**Ready in:** 1 hr. 45 minutes | **Serving:** 4)

**Ingredients**

- Lemon zest: 1 teaspoon

- ¾ cup of non-fat plain Greek yogurt

- Fresh lemon juice: 2 tablespoons

- Chopped fresh oregano: 1 tablespoon

- Or dried oregano: 1 teaspoon

- ¼ of a teaspoon crushed red pepper

- Half of a teaspoon salt, divided

- Two whole-wheat pita bread: 6 and 1/2 inch each halved

- Chopped fresh mint: 2 teaspoons

- Extra virgin olive oil: 5 teaspoons divided

- Chopped fresh dill: 2 teaspoons

- Ground pepper: 1 teaspoon

- Minced garlic: 2 and ¾ teaspoons divided

- One and ½ English cucumber halved, seeded, grated and half of it sliced

- 4 leaves of lettuce

- 1 cup diced plum tomatoes

- Half of a cup thinly sliced red onion

- 4 cups of chicken tenders

## Instructions

1. Add lemon juice, oregano, lemon zest, three tsp. of extra virgin olive oil, crushed red pepper, and 2 tsp. of garlic in a big bowl and mix properly.

2. Then add in the chicken and mix well with the mixture prepared before.

3. Let it Marinate in the refrigerator for one hour for the minimum or four hours.

4. In the meantime, mix 1/4 tsp. of salt with grated cucumber in a fine sieve. For 15 minutes, let it drain, then squeeze to get as much liquid out as possible.

5.  Add to a bowl then add in dill, yogurt, fresh ground black pepper, mint, and the remaining two tsp. of oil, 1/4 tsp. salt, 3/4 tsp. of garlic. Let it cool in the refrigerator.

6.  Let your grill pre-heat on high.

7.  Grease the grill rack with oil. Grill the chicken for almost four minutes each side, or until an instant-read thermometer when inserted in the chicken center will show 165 F.

8.  For serving, put the sauce inside each pita pocket.

9.  Add in the red onion, grilled chicken, sliced cucumber, lettuce, and tomatoes.

10. Serve hot and enjoy.

**Nutritional value**: Calories 271 | Fat 8.6g | Carbs 33.3g | Protein 37.5 g

# Mediterranean Dinner Recipes

Some delicious, healthy, and hearty Mediterranean diets dinner recipes are as follow.

## 1.Slow Cooker Kale and Turkey Meatball Soup

(**Ready in:** 4 hr. 15 minutes | **Serving:** 4)

**Ingredients**

- 4 cups of lean ground turkey (85% lean)

- Bread: 2 slices

- Kale: 4 cups

- ¼ of a cup milk

- Two cloves of garlic pressed

- One medium shallot finely diced

- ½ of a teaspoon freshly grated nutmeg

- One teaspoon of oregano

- 1/4 of a teaspoon red pepper flakes

- Italian parsley chopped: 2 tablespoons

- Two carrots cut in slices

- One egg beat

- One tablespoon of olive oil

- Chicken or vegetable broth: 8 cups

- One can of 15- ounce white Northern beans rinsed, drained

- Half yellow onion finely diced

- Half of a cup Parmigiano-Reggiano grated, extra for garnish

- Kosher salt and freshly ground pepper

**Instructions**

1. In a large mixing bowl, add milk, cut the bread into pieces, and let it soak in milk. Add the garlic, turkey, nutmeg, shallot, red pepper flakes, salt, oregano, pepper, egg, cheese, and parsley. Mix carefully with your hands. Use a scooper to make half-inch balls.

2. Put a wide skillet on medium flame, heat the olive oil, then sear the meatballs gently on every side for two minutes. Turn off the heat and set it aside.

3. Add the onion, stock, beans, kale, and carrots to a 5 to 7 quarter slow cooker.

4. Add meatballs the kale, and cook for four hours at low or until the meatballs start floating to the top.

5. Garnish the soup with Parmesan grated cheese, red pepper flakes, and fresh leaves of parsley.

**Nutritional value**: Calories 250 | Fat 23 g | Carbs 20.3 g | Protein 14,4 g

6. Heat one tbsp. of extra virgin olive oil over medium flame in the skillet. Add onion and cook until transparent, for three minutes.

7. Add the remaining ingredients for the rice and the marinade reserve.

8. Let the liquid boil and then let it simmer for 30 seconds.

9. Put the chicken on top of the rice, then cover the skillet. Let it bake for 35 minutes after removing the cover and bake for another ten minutes, or until all the moisture is absorbed and the rice is soft.

10. Remove from the oven and, if necessary, allow to rest for ten minutes before serving, garnished with oregano parsley and fresh lemon zest.

**Nutritional value**: Calories 323 | Fat 21 g | Carbs 33 g | Protein 18 g

# 3.Greek Turkey Meatball Gyro with Tzatziki

(**Ready in:** 30 minutes | **Serving:** 3)

## Ingredients

- Extra-virgin olive oil: 2 tablespoons

- Ground turkey: 4 cups

- Finely chopped red onion: 1/4 cup

- Two cloves of minced garlic

- Chopped fresh spinach: 1 cup

- Kosher salt

- Freshly ground black pepper to season

- Oregano: 1 teaspoon

## Instructions

1. Add diced red onion, ground turkey, oregano, sliced garlic, spinach, salt pepper to a big bowl, and mix well. Mix into sticky dough balls with your hands.

2. Again, with your hands, make the mixture into smaller balls of one inch each.

3. Heat a skillet on high flame. Put olive oil in the pan, then stir in the meatballs. Cook each side for about three minutes, until all surfaces are well browned. Turn off the heat and let it rest.

4. Meanwhile, add lemon juice, Greek yogurt, dill, grated cucumber, salt, and garlic powder. Mix it well until well combined.

5. Add three meatballs, tomato, cucumber, and sliced red onion to a flatbread.

6. Drizzle the sauce over and serve with lemon wedges.

**Nutritional value**: Calories 216 | Fat 3 g | Carbs 32 g | Protein 22 g

# 4.Shrimp, Avocado and Feta Wrap

(**Ready in:** 10 minutes | **Serving:** 1)

Ingredients

- One whole-wheat tortilla

- Chopped cooked shrimp: 6 tbsp.

- ¼ of a cup of chopped tomato

- One scallion (sliced)

- ¼ of a cup of chopped avocado

- Crumbled feta cheese: 2 tablespoons

- Lime juice: 1 tablespoon

Instructions

1. In a big mixing bowl, add shrimp, tomato, lime juice, avocado, feta, and scallion and mix well.

2. Lay tortilla flat on the serving plate, add the shrimp mix in it.

3. Fold the tortilla and serve right away with lime wedges.

**Nutritional value**: Calories 371 | Fat 13.7g | Carbs 34.3g | Protein 28.8g

# 5.Provençal Baked Fish with Roasted Potatoes and Mushroom

(**Ready in**: about 60 minutes | **Serving:** 4)

## Ingredients

- Yukon Gold potatoes cubed: 4 cups

- Olive oil divided: two tbsp.

- Salt: ¼ tsp.

- Herbs: 1 tsp.

- Mushrooms: 4 cups (sliced)

- Two cloves garlic (sliced)

- Lemon juice: 4 tbsp.

- Ground pepper: ¼ tsp.

- Thyme

- Halibut: 1 and ½ cup, cut into four pieces

## Instructions

1. Let the oven heat till 425 F.

2. Add one tbsp. of oil, potatoes, mushroom, pepper, and salt in a bowl.

3. Transfer it to a baking dish and roast for almost forty minutes until the vegetables are soft. Stir the vegetables and add garlic.

4. Place fish over it. Drizzle with one tbsp. of oil, lemon juice. Sprinkle with herbs and bake till fish is flaky for fifteen minutes.

**Nutritional value**: Calories 276 | Fat 18.8g | Carbs 25.3g | Protein 24.4g

# 6.Salmon Bowl with Farro, Black Beans, and Tahini Dressing

(**Ready in:** 20 minutes | **Serving:** 2)

## Ingredients

- Half of a cup cooked black beans

- Salmon: 3/4 cup

- Tahini: 2 tablespoons

- Zest and juice of one lemon

- ¼ of teaspoon garlic powder

- Half teaspoon of turmeric (divided)

- Farro: ¼ cup

- Half of teaspoon cumin

- One and ½ teaspoons smoked paprika

- Two scallions, thinly chopped

- Half a tsp. of coriander

- Four pieces Boston lettuce leaves

- Thinly sliced half avocado

- Extra-virgin olive oil: 6 tablespoons (divided)

- Fresno Chile: ¼ of a whole, thinly sliced

- Kosher salt and freshly ground black pepper

## Instructions

1. Mix lemon zest, the tahini, lemon juice, garlic powder, and 1/4 teaspoon of turmeric and a big bowl.

2. Slowly add three tablespoons of olive oil and mix until smooth and fully emulsified for the sauce. Adjust salt and pepper.

3. Put a small pot over medium flame, add the farro and one cup of water. Let it boil. Lower the heat and let it simmer for 20 - 25 minutes until the farro is soft. Set it aside.

4. In a bowl, add one tablespoon of olive oil, the beans, and the cumin. Mix well set it aside.

5. Mix smoked paprika, 1/4 teaspoon of turmeric, coriander, salt, and pepper and season the salmon with this mix.

6. Heat the remaining two tablespoons of olive oil over a low flame in a medium skillet. Add in the salmon and cook for

about five minutes until lightly browned on one side and opaque in the middle.

7. Lay lettuce leaves at the bottom of a serving bowl. Add farro, salmon, and black beans. Garnish with the slices of avocado, the scallions, and the diced chili. Add dressing on top.

**Nutritional value**: Calories 732 | Fat 37 g | Carbs 41 g | Protein 39 g

# 7.Spinach, Feta and Artichoke Matzo Mina

(**Ready in:** 45 minutes | **Serving:** 2)

**Ingredients**

- 1 tbsp. olive oil

- Two large eggs

- Three sheets of matzo

- 1/4 cup of crumbled feta cheese

- 3/4 of a cup low-fat cottage cheese

- 1/4 cup fresh dill (chopped)

- 1/4 tsp. crushed red pepper flakes

- 3/4 of a cup of frozen or canned artichoke hearts plain, unmarinated

- Kosher salt to taste (as needed)

- 4 and 1/4 tablespoon of fresh spinach roughly chopped

- Scallions (chopped)

- 1 tsp. lemon zest

## Instructions

1. Let the oven preheat to 350 F and oil a 9 by 9 baking dish (square).

2. Halve the artichokes. Put a large skillet over medium flame. Add artichoke in it and sauté them till they are brown. Turn off the heat and set them aside.

3. Add cottage cheese, lemon zest, scallions, spinach, crushed red pepper, and dill in a big mixing bowl and mix well.

4. Gradually add feta cheese, one handful at a time. This filling should be smooth and creamy with a hint of tang and a tad bit salty.

5. Be careful not to add too much feta or the filling will be very salty. But if after adding all the feta, it is not salty to your liking, then add more salt.

6. After adjusting the salt, add two beaten eggs and mix well.

7. Add matzo sheets in water to soften them but do not make them too soft.

8. Lay a matzo sheet on the bottom of the prepared baking dish. Cover the whole baking dish's base.

9. Add feta cheese filling on top of matzo and half of the artichoke (sautéed) hearts.

10. Then add another layer of matzo, the rest of the cheese filling, and the rest of the artichoke sautéed hearts.

11. Cover the whole thing with matzo sheets. It will shrink up, so be generous with the matzo sheets.

12. You may add a spinach layer in between fillings.

13. Beat an egg and brush it over the matzo layer.

14. Let it bake for 45 minutes.

15. The top layer will be golden brown.

16. Take it out of the oven, let it sit for five minutes, then cut pieces, and serve right away and enjoy.

**Nutritional value**: Calories 234 | Fat 13 g | Carbs 21 g | Protein 14 g

# 8.Swordfish with Olives, Capers and Tomatoes over Polenta

(**Ready in:** 45 minutes | **Serving:** 4)

## Ingredients

- Capers: 1 tablespoon rinsed

- Chopped fresh basil: 3 tablespoons

- Swordfish: 4 cups, cut into four steaks

- Two and ½ cups of water

- Extra-virgin olive oil: 1 tablespoon

- A pinch of crushed red pepper

- Half teaspoon of salt (divided)

- Two cloves of pressed garlic

- For garnish, fresh basil

- Half cup of regular or coarse yellow cornmeal

- Four medium stalks of celery, chopped

- ¼ of cup green olives pitted and roughly diced

- One can of 15 ounces of unsalted chopped tomatoes

- Freshly ground black pepper: ⅛ teaspoon

## Instructions

1. Put a saucepan over medium flame and boil two cups of water with 1/4 tsp. of salt. Add the cornmeal carefully to avoid any lumps.

2. Cook for three minutes, keep stirring.

3. Lower the heat. Stir after every five minutes, cook for 20-25 minutes. If it becomes too hard, add a half cup of water, turn off the heat but keep it covered.

4. In the meantime, in a large skillet over a medium flame, add in the oil. Add celery fry it, frequently stirring, until soft, for around five minutes.

5. Then add garlic, cook for almost 30 seconds. Add in olives, tomatoes, basil, crushed red pepper, capers, freshly ground black pepper, and the remaining 1/4 tsp. of sea salt.

6. Cover it lower the heat, and cook for five minutes.

7. Add swordfish in the sauce. Let it simmer, and cover it cook for 10-15 minutes, until swordfish is cooked completely.

8. On a serving tray, layer the cornmeal at the bottom. Add the fish over the cornmeal, cover with the sauce and, garnish with fresh basil, serve hot and enjoy.

**Nutritional value**: Calories 276 | Fat 12.1 g | Carbs 18.9 g | Protein 22 g

# 9.Greek Lemon Chicken Skewers with Tzatziki Sauce

(**Ready in:** 30 minutes | **Serving:** 4)

**Ingredients**

- Cauliflower rice: 4 cups

- Seven tablespoons of extra virgin olive oil

- ⅓ of a cup chopped red onion

- Half of a cup chopped fresh dill (divided)

- 4 cups of boneless, skinless chicken breasts

- ¾ of a teaspoon salt (divided)

- Lemon juice: 3 tablespoons

- Diced Kalamata olives: 2 tablespoons

- Dried oregano: 1 teaspoon

- One cup of halved cherry tomatoes

- Crumbled feta cheese: 2 tablespoons

- One cup of diced cucumber

- Lemon wedges for serving

- Half teaspoon of freshly ground black pepper (divided)

**Instructions**

1. Preheat grill to medium.

2. Put a large skillet over a medium flame add two tbsp. of oil in it and heat. Add cauliflower, 1/4 teaspoon of sea salt and onion, often stir and cook until the cauliflower is tender, for about five minutes. Turn off the heat and add in 1/4 cup of dill.

3. In the meantime, rub one teaspoon of extra virgin olive oil all over the chicken. Add 1/4 teaspoon of salt and 1/4 teaspoon of freshly ground black pepper. Grill it, flip once. If an instant-read thermometer is inserted into the thickest part of the chicken, it will read 165 degrees F in about 15 minutes. Transfer chicken to a clean cutting surface and cut into slices.

4. In the meantime, in a small mixing bowl, add four tablespoons of oil, remaining 1/4 teaspoon each salt and pepper, oregano, lemon juice and mix well.

5. Take four serving bowls, add cauliflower rice at the bottom. Add the chicken slices, feta, tomatoes, cucumber, and olives.

6. Add 1/4 cup of dill on top. Also, drizzle the vinaigrette on top.

7.  Serve hot with lemon wedges.

**Nutritional value**: Calories 425 | Fat 20 g | Carbs 19 g | Protein 31 g

# 10.Mediterranean Veggie Wrap with Cilantro Hummus

(**Ready in:** 20 minutes | **Serving:** 4)

**Ingredients**

**Cilantro Hummus**

- One can of chickpeas

- 15 ounces unsalted garbanzo beans

- Extra virgin olive oil: 2 tablespoons

- ¼ of a teaspoon white pepper

- Tahini: 1 tablespoon

- ¼ of a teaspoon salt

- One clove of garlic (peeled)

- ¼ of a cup fresh cilantro

- Lemon juice: 3 tablespoons

**Mediterranean Wraps**

- Light oval multi-grain wraps: 4 pieces (tomato-flavored)

- Baby greens: 4 cups (mixed)

- One clove of minced garlic

- Half cup red onion (thinly sliced)

- ¼ of a cup of crumbled feta cheese (reduced-fat)

- Half large cucumber: one cup, halved lengthwise and sliced

- Bottled banana peppers (mild): 2 tablespoons, sliced

- Diced tomato: 1 cup

- Extra-virgin olive oil: one tablespoon

- Balsamic vinegar: 1 tablespoon

- ¼ of a teaspoon freshly ground black pepper

**Instructions**

1. Add peeled garlic in a food processor and mince it.

2. Wash and drain the can packed chickpeas. In a processor, add three tbsp. of lemon juice, two tbsp. of olive oil, garbanzo beans, one tbsp. tahini, 1/4 of a teaspoon of sea salt, 1/4 of a tsp. of pepper.

3. Pulse on high until smooth. Clean up the food processor's bowl as often as needed. Then add 1/4 of cup fresh cilantro leaves.

4. Pulse it again several times. Cilantro will evenly distribute and chop with the mixture.

5. Keep in the refrigerator until ready to serve.

6. Meanwhile, add cucumber, red onion, banana peppers, feta cheese, greens, tomato in a big mixing bowl.

7. In a small mixing bowl, add olive oil, freshly ground black pepper, vinegar, garlic, and whisk until completely emulsified.

8. Add this dressing to the greens mixture. Mix well.

9. Lay flat the wraps on the serving tray and spread two and a half tbsp. of hummus on each wrap. Add green mixture doused in sauce on top. Roll up like a burrito, serve right away and enjoy.

**Nutritional value**: Calories 268 | Fat 12.2g | Carbs 36.1g | Protein 15.2g

# 11.Pesto Quinoa Bowls with Roasted Veggies and Labneh

(**Ready in:** about 50 min | **Servings:** 4)

**Ingredients**

- Labneh or non-fat plain Greek yogurt: 1 cup

- Extra-virgin olive oil

- One large Japanese eggplant (diced)

- One pint of halved cherry tomatoes

- A handful of Romano or green beans

- Quinoa: 1 cup rinsed

- One medium zucchini (cubed)

- Half of a cup of pesto

- One garlic clove (pressed)

- Juice from half a lemon

- A handful of cilantro and parsley (roughly sliced)

- Kosher salt and freshly ground black pepper

**Instructions**

1. Let the oven pre-heat to 400F.

2. Put parchment paper on a large baking sheet and place the cherry tomatoes, eggplant, beans, and zucchini on it.

3. Put the olive oil over vegetables and add salt and pepper. Roast for 30-40 minutes, until all vegetables are soft and caramelized.

4. Meanwhile, in a saucepan, add the quinoa with two cups of water and a pinch of salt. Let it boil, then cover it, simmer for 15 minutes.

5. After you have cooked the quinoa, uncover it, fluff it with a fork and let it cool. When the quinoa has moderately cooled, mix it with pesto.

6. In a small bowl, add the garlic, lemon juice, herbs, and labneh and mix well.

7. In each bowl, add quinoa, mix veggies, and a spoonful of labneh on the side.

8. Serve right away and enjoy.

**Nutritional value**: Calories 362 | Fat 42 g | Carbs 96 g | Protein 23 g

# Conclusion

In the modern world, we conceive the term "diet" is about the pressure or restriction that makes you lose the desired weight. This Mediterranean diet may be the farthest from that concept. It is a heart-healthy diet that includes the food from people living in the Mediterranean Sea area, such as Italy, Greece, and Croatia. These people incorporate a plant-based diet, full of nutrients in their meals. The meals are filled with leafy greens and healthy fats like omega-3 fatty acids (fish oil) and olive oil. It is a diet that is considered to be heart-healthy. Mediterranean diet is abundant in vegetables and herbs, whole grains, fish, nuts, olive oil, and legumes. But you must exclude dairy, red meat, and sugar foods and on this diet (although limited quantities of yogurt and cheese are encouraged).

The true Mediterranean diet is more than simply consuming healthy, wholesome food. Every day physical exercise and food preparation and sharing are essential components of the Mediterranean Diet Pyramid. Following this will have a positive impact on your attitude and mental wellbeing and help cultivate a deep enjoyment of the benefits of consuming nutritious and tasty foods.

Of course, it is never easy to make adjustments to your lifestyle, particularly if you are attempting to stay away from the comfort of packaged and processed foods. But the Mediterranean diet can be both a cost-effective pleasant change and a very safe form of living. It may take some time to turn from pepperoni and spaghetti to salmon and avocados, but you will quickly be on the road to a better, healthy, and long life.

You can switch to a Mediterranean diet by adding these themes to your daily routine:

- **Eating lots of vegetables**

- **Always eating healthy breakfast**

- **Eating seafood at least twice a week**

- **Cooking a vegetarian meal one day of the week**

- **By enjoying dairy products in balance**

- **By eating fresh fruit instead of sweets**

- **Using plant-based good fats**

  The Mediterranean diet is more than a simple diet. It is a lifestyle. By following this lifestyle, you can get the benefits like:

- It helps to promote safe cholesterol levels in the body.

- It enhances your body's capacity to consume blood sugar (prediabetes and diabetes can endanger the health of your heart).

- The most important benefit is the Mediterranean diet fights off the harmful inflammation, a reaction caused by the immune system as the body attacks potential intruders. Acute, or just one time, inflammation is effective in the battle against viruses and pathogens. Still, obese individuals that eat excessive amounts of processed carbohydrates and have a poor diet can have persistent inflammation that may contribute to diabetes, heart, and liver disease.

- It makes the arteries remain stable and does not let plaque buildups.

In summary, the Mediterranean diet is nothing more than healthy for you and your dear ones. In the long run, your heart will be thankful and help you live a long, healthy life.